1D

ONE DIRECTION

BEHIND THE SCENES

One Direction: Behind the Scenes

Copyright © 2011 by One Direction
All rights reserved. Printed in the United States of America. No part of this book may be used or
reproduced in any manner whatsoever without written permission except in the case of brief quotations
embodied in critical articles and reviews. For information address HarperCollins Children's Books, a
division of HarperCollins Publishers, 10 East 53rd Street, New York, NY 10022.
www.harpercollinschildrens.com
Library of Congress Cataloging-in-Publication data is available.
ISBN 978-0-06-222315-9

Text by Sarah Delmege
Design by Wayne Redwood
Production by Sian Smith
Photography by Simon Harris

12 13 14 15 16   LP/RRDW   10 9 8 7 6 5 4 3 2 1
❖
Originally published by HarperCollins UK in 2011

1D
ONE DIRECTION

BEHIND THE SCENES

HARPER
An Imprint of HarperCollins Publishers

1D ONE DIRECTION

CONTENTS

How It All Began	8
The Making of One Direction	18
Our Great Big One Direction Quiz	22
Life After *The X Factor*	24
Boy Bonding!	26
All Access One Direction	28
One Direction Style Guide	32
Baby Photos - Guess Who	36
Who Said What?	38
Hanging with One Direction	40
Who's Your Favorite?	48
A Date with 1D	52
Live Your Life the 1D Way!	54
One Direction and You	56
The Future	58

HOW IT ALL BEGAN

The band opens their photo albums and shares their childhood stories.

Liam

Name: Liam James Payne
Born: August 29, 1993
Star sign: Virgo
Hometown: Wolverhampton, England
Eye color: Brown
Fave aftershave: Paco Rabanne's 1 million
Fave grooming product: Hair wax
Best thing about being in One Direction: There's never a dull moment

Finding his voice

"I first started singing when I was about six. We used to go to my grandad's in Cornwall or to holiday camps and I used to sing on the karaoke all the time. My favorite track to perform was Robbie Williams's 'Angels.'"

Childhood dreams

"At one stage I wanted to become a boxer. I used to box three times a week, but I had to give that up for *The X Factor*, as you can't turn up on stage with bruises."

Never giving up

"I was 14 when I first auditioned for *The X Factor* back in 2008, but Simon didn't take me through because he didn't think I was ready for it. It was a terrible disappointment, but I was up against a lot of stiff competition. And looking back, I'm thankful that I didn't get through, otherwise I wouldn't be in One Direction now."

The boys on Liam

Louis: "I think Liam's the sensible one."

Zayn: "He's not just the dad of the group, he's the grandad of the group! Being in the group's been good for him because he's become more immature. Before, he thought he was about 30!"

Liam: "Grandad? I suppose I'm the sensible one. We all love to have a laugh and it's great fun to be in One Direction but sometimes you gotta have your Mr. Serious head on!"

Louis

Name: Louis William Tomlinson
Born: December 24, 1991
Star sign: Capricorn
Home town: Doncaster, England
Eye color: Blue
Fave aftershave: Hollister
Fave grooming product: Dry shampoo – when I can't be bothered to wash my hair
Best thing about being in One Direction: Just the laugh we have. And also, I've made four new friends.

Mr. Tomlinson, sir

"Since the age of 13, I've wanted to be an actor or a singer. I always had a backup plan though - because I love kids, I decided it would be great to be a teacher. It would have been funny if Zayn and I had somehow ended up on the same course."

Taste of fame

"I posted some clips on YouTube of me singing songs like The Fray's 'Look After You' when I was about 15 or 16, to try and get some kind of feedback. There's also a video on there of me performing as Danny in my school's production of *Grease*. I loved being in that show, it was such a laugh, and I was really pleased to land the role of Danny as it was the first show I'd auditioned for."

Fortune-teller

"A lot of kids complain about school, but I actually enjoyed it and I really miss it now. I remember one of my teachers saying to me when I was about 15, 'I can tell by your personality that you're going to go on to do big things.'"

The boys on Louis

Zayn: "He's the joker! People always say Harry or Niall are the Robbie of the group but behind the scenes, it's always Louis. He's very much a rule breaker, doesn't like to stick to the rules."

Louis: "When we have to be professional I can be serious but I LOVE to have a laugh."

Harry

Name: Harry Edward Styles
Born: February 1, 1994
Star sign: Aquarius
Hometown: Cheshire, England
Eye color: Green
Fave aftershave: Bleu de Chanel
Fave grooming product: Shampoo – I use L'Oréal Elvive
Best thing about being in One Direction: The four guys that I'm with

Born performer

"I started singing in primary school and was always in plays and shows, so I was performing from a young age. All I ever wanted to do was something that was well paid. I really liked the idea of being a singer, but I had no idea how to go about it."

Early fame

"I formed a band called White Eskimo with some school friends. We performed locally and also won a battle of the bands competition. Winning that and playing to a lot of people really showed me that singing was what I wanted to do. I got such a thrill when I was in front of people that it made me want to do it more and more."

Thanks, Mom!

"My mom is always telling me that I'm a good singer and it was her who put the *X Factor* application in for me. Obviously, I was hopeful that the judges would like me as well. It would have been a major setback in my plans for world domination if they hadn't."

The boys on Harry

Niall: "Curly!"

Louis: "He's the cheeky one, definitely."

Niall: "And he's also curly."

Louis: "He's a massive flirt but also a great friend to all of us, very easy to talk to."

Zayn

Name: Zayn Jawaad Malik
Born: January 12, 1993
Star sign: Capricorn
Hometown: Bradford, England
Eye color: Hazel
Fave aftershave: Unforgivable by Sean John
Fave grooming product: Hair wax
Best thing about being in One Direction: All the free clothes and I get to do what I love every day

Larger than life

"I've always been the loud one in my house. In fact, I was so hyperactive that once my mom even took me to the doctor."

A different direction

"I've acted since I was 12 and I've been in a lot of shows because I was at a performing arts school. When I was younger, I always wanted to be an actor, but I also really liked the idea of becoming a drama teacher. Louis and I are very similar like that – he wanted to do the same."

High hopes

"I remember my drama teacher telling me that if I carried on and worked hard I could really make something of myself, but I thought she probably said that to everyone so I took it with a pinch of salt."

The boys on Zayn

Louis: "If I wanna break the rules or start being mischievous, he's the one to do it with."
Zayn: "No I'm not!"
Liam: "Zayn's quite quiet as well. When he first meets someone he's not as chatty."
Zayn: "I was shy before the competition but now that I've been with the boys I've come out of my shell a bit."

Niall

Name: Niall James Horan
Born: September 13, 1993
Star sign: Virgo
Hometown: Westmeath, Ireland
Eye color: Blue
Fave aftershave: Armani Mania
Fave grooming product: L'Oréal Homme wax and clay
Best thing about being in One Direction: That we all get along

Small town, big dreams

"The town where I live is really nice but quite small and there isn't much for young people to do. I love playing guitar and I spent most of my time just hanging out with my friends or singing, and obviously all that singing is what led me to *The X Factor*."

Talent spotted

"When I went to secondary school, everyone realized that I could sing, so I started entering talent shows and even won a few of them here and there. While I was doing one of the talent shows, a guy asked me if I wanted to take part in a local Stars in Their Eyes-type competition. Although I didn't win, I got a lot of good local press, which was pretty cool."

The boys on Niall

Harry: "Niall's the one that we all envy because he gets to be really immature because he has a babyface. I'm the youngest, but everyone thinks he is."
Liam: "He's very carefree. I'd call him a free spirit."

THE MAKING OF ONE DIRECTION

How the legend began...

It seems strange now to think that the boys haven't always been in a group. They each came to *The X Factor* as nervous solo artists, hoping against hope that this could be the day that their lives changed beyond all recognition. They all knew how important the auditions were. After all, there are TV shows and TV shows, but *The X Factor* is very special. Every wannabe singer in the UK would love to be on it.

But things didn't go according to plan. Although all five boys performed very strongly and the judges liked them, it was felt they all lacked experience. And at the final stage it seemed like it was all over when the boys were told they hadn't gotten through. They were gutted. Their dreams in tatters, they left the stage. Then someone said they wanted the guys on stage because the judges had an announcement to make. Harry, Louis, Liam, Niall and Zayn had no idea what was coming next.

Liam says, "When Nicole told us that she thought we were too talented to let us go and they wanted us to form a group, my head started spinning. She said, 'You're going to get the chance to see what it's like to be a group.' Then Simon told us that they'd decided to put us through to the Judges' Houses and we had a real shot at the competition. I don't think any of us knew what to say."

"I was crying like a little baby." Louis grins, laughing at the memory.

The boys screamed and hugged each other, jumping up and down in excitement. But moments later reality hit. Being in a band was a risk. What happened if they didn't get on?

"When Simon told us that we were going to be part of a group, I whooped. And then I panicked. What if there was one person we didn't get on with?" Harry remembers.

There was no precedent for this. It had never happened before. The boys were making *X Factor* history. But as the guys looked at each other, they all knew they were prepared to do whatever it took to get their chance.

Decision made, there was one thing they had to do and quickly. Find a name. The boys came up with lots of different ideas, but none of them seemed quite right. Then Harry had an idea. "We've all wanted the same thing from the start, so I came up with the name One Direction."

As soon as Niall, Liam, Louis and Zayn heard it, they loved it. It just sounded right for them. It summed up exactly what they were about and it sounded good. One Direction it was to be. And they certainly made their impact on the show. From the very beginning it was obvious that the boys had exactly the right attitude. And they were now all dedicated to making the group a success. And that's what it takes to make it to the top: talent, hard work, team spirit and most of all, a positive attitude. The world had better get ready: One Direction had arrived.

One Direction it was to be.

OUR GREAT BIG ONE DIRECTION QUIZ

Think you know 1D inside out? Take our superfan quiz and find out...

Round one Totally trivia!

1. What did Louis want to be when he grew up?
   A. Famous
   B. Power Ranger
   C. Racing driver
   D. Stuntman

2. What's Harry's sister called?
   A. Rachel
   B. Lizzie
   C. Lauren
   D. Gemma

3. What did Niall sing in a local talent competition?
   A. "I'm Yours"
   B. "You're the One That I Want"
   C. "Poker Face"
   D. "Cry Me a River"

4. What was the name of Zayn's first pet?
   A. Rover
   B. Curly
   C. Bubbles
   D. Tyson

5. What was Liam's performing arts group called?
   A. Green Door
   B. Blue Post
   C. Pink Productions
   D. Sparkle Performers

Round two
Say what?

Fill in the missing words!

1. "I felt like if I'd sung I would have been _____. I didn't understand it." – Harry (when he was struck by stage fright)

2. "I'm not like people think I am. I know I'm a bit _____ sometime but I do work hard." – Louis

3. "Now I've got a _____ chance, I'm not going to blow it." – Liam

4. "I'm not one of those people who have loads of _____." – Zayn

5. "We want to _____ people. We want them to know we're not your normal boy band." – Niall

Round three Name these X Factor tunes.

1. Who sang "Isn't She Lovely" by Stevie Wonder at his audition?
2. Which song did the boys sing with Robbie?
3. Which song did the boys sing in the first live X Factor show?
4. Which Rihanna song did the boys cover?
5. What would have been the guys' "Winner's Single"?

Round four One Direction math!

1. What year did the boys compete on The X Factor?
2. What year was Harry born?
3. How many acts went through to Boot Camp?
4. How many acts from each category went to the Judges' Houses?
5. How many weeks of the live shows did One Direction appear in?

Answers

Round one
1. B. Power Ranger
2. D. Gemma
3. A. "I'm Yours"
4. D. Tyson
5. C. Pink

Round two
1. Sick
2. Mad
3. Second
4. Friends
5. Surprise Productions

Round three
1. Harry
2. "She's the One"
3. Coldplay's
4. "Only Girl (in the World)"
5. "Forever Young"

Round four
1. 2010
2. 1994
3. 100
4. 8
5. 10

BOY BONDING!

The boys have really learned how to get on as a band.

So... tell us about your friendship!

Zayn: "When we're not together, we all text each other saying, 'Hey, I miss you.' That sounds really girlie, but that level of closeness is important."

Liam: "It's crazy how close we are. At Christmas, I missed Harry wandering around naked and Niall farting all the time."

Louis: "I love all the guys, but Harry and I are like actual best friends. We have a lot in common, so we pair up for hotel rooms and taxis. I feel sorry for people who do all this on their own."

Niall: "We are all so close! We are literally five best friends.... We laugh all the time! And there is so much banter it will be impossible for any of us to get cocky!"

Louis: "We were always looking after each other from the word 'go.'"

Do you all have different roles in the band?

Liam: "It will usually be Louis and me kicking people up the backside when we need to laugh. We sort of work as a team. But Niall just loves to have a laugh 24/7."

Louis: "His memory is terrible. He's like a goldfish."

Niall: "That's not fair."

Harry: "Oh it is."

Louis: "Harry is like the balance in the middle. He'll mess around but he will work. He knows where the line is. If there's ever a band argument, he's like the peacemaker too. On camera Zayn is quite shy, but in real life he's not like that at all. He's come out of his shell so much."

Zayn: "The funny thing is, I've always been quite loud. But for some reason on TV it seems like I'm the quiet one. Probably because this lot is so loud."

What's the silliest argument One Direction has ever had?

Louis: "Probably when me and Zayn argued over FIFA on the PlayStation the other day. You know what guys are like when they get competitive. But we never hold a grudge and we were fine five minutes later."

Niall: "When we were on *The X Factor* we argued over stupid things like: 'Why are you wearing my shoes?' But that was 'cause we were so tired all the time. To be honest, we don't really argue at all."

Zayn: "The silliest thing me and Louis have ever argued over was, believe it or not, a plastic bag! But it lasted for about two seconds and we were cool after."

Harry: "I think it's over the PlayStation – about who's better than who."

Who has the most annoying habits?

Louis: "Harry sometimes sleeptalks, which was very strange the first time he did it. But now I've started sleeptalking and sleepwalking as well, so it's a bit crazy."

Niall: "Liam and Zayn are pretty good – it's Louis and Harry who make all the noise! Although Zayn always looks in the mirror, which can be quite annoying."

Zayn: "Liam hasn't got any bad habits, which is why I like sharing with him. Harry snores, though."

Harry: "Apparently I sleepwalk and sleeptalk. I'm going to purchase the sleeptalking app for my phone so I can see if it's true. As for the others, Louis is always fiddling with his hair. Does that count?"

Liam: "For me, it's got to be Niall. He's always farting!"

"It's crazy how close we are."

ALL ACCESS ONE DIRECTION

Fourteen things you didn't know about the guys.

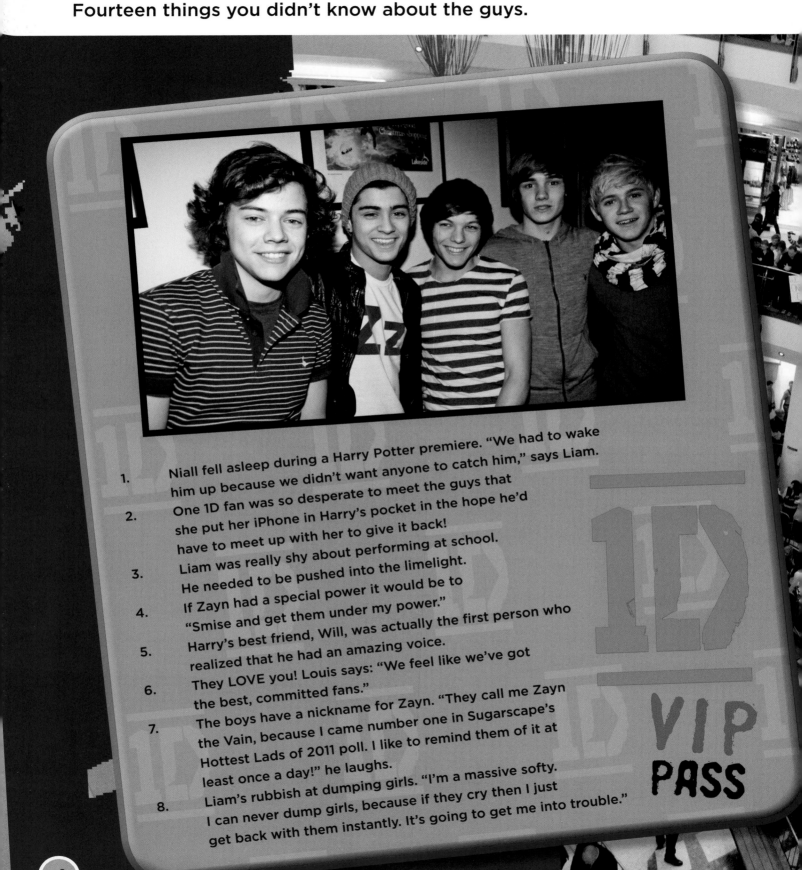

1. Niall fell asleep during a Harry Potter premiere. "We had to wake him up because we didn't want anyone to catch him," says Liam.

2. One 1D fan was so desperate to meet the guys that she put her iPhone in Harry's pocket in the hope he'd have to meet up with her to give it back!

3. Liam was really shy about performing at school. He needed to be pushed into the limelight.

4. If Zayn had a special power it would be to "Smise and get them under my power."

5. Harry's best friend, Will, was actually the first person who realized that he had an amazing voice.

6. They LOVE you! Louis says: "We feel like we've got the best, committed fans."

7. The boys have a nickname for Zayn. "They call me Zayn the Vain, because I came number one in Sugarscape's Hottest Lads of 2011 poll. I like to remind them of it at least once a day!" he laughs.

8. Liam's rubbish at dumping girls. "I'm a massive softy. I can never dump girls, because if they cry then I just get back with them instantly. It's going to get me into trouble."

VIP PASS

9. Louis owns boxers with 'lubbly jubbly' written on them!

10. Liam used to practice kissing on the back of his hand!

11. Niall is great at accents. His dad thinks he can probably do a better Geordie accent than Cheryl Cole!

12. They may sizzle on stage, but the boys aren't so hot in the kitchen. "Harry nearly burned the house down the other day," laughs Niall.

13. Zayn's first kiss was when he was just ten years old. "She was taller than me, I had to stand on a ledge to reach her."

14. Louis currently has the biggest biceps in the group. "I can't stop flexing them. Mostly in Liam's face."

1D

VIP PASS

ONE DIRECTION STYLE GUIDE

Following fashion and looking on trend is very important for the 1D guys. And part of being in a band is having to combine everyone's fashion style and come up with a unified look. As Harry explains: "We all wanted to keep our individuality, but we needed to look like a band as well, so we kind of got twists on the looks we already had."

And they have pulled it off brilliantly! Although they look very much like a group, you can still see flashes of the guys' true personalities. Harry still shows the same sense of style he had at his very first audition and Niall will often wear a buttoned-up shirt.

And the boys definitely use clothes to show off their personalities. Who can forget the time that Louis was spotted leaving the studio in a hospital gown? Or the all-in-ones that the guys have been photographed in?

Costumes aside, One Direction's style varies with every member from preppy to savvy, from cute to boy next door. No matter whether they're suited and booted or in flip-flops they somehow manage to look cool without appearing like they're trying too hard!

"We all wanted to keep our individuality."

STYLE FILE

The boys reveal all about their style!

Zayn: "Yep, I'm vain. It doesn't take me long to get ready, but once I'm out, I have to keep checking everything's in place."

Who takes the longest to get ready?

Harry: "Zayn takes the longest!"

Zayn: "I don't take the longest!"

Harry: "With your makeup?"

Zayn: "OK, I admit I probably enjoy it the most, but I don't take the longest!"

What are your top tips for looking good?

Niall: "Wearing bracelets can snazz up any kind of outfit. As can a watch. They do a lot."

Zayn: "Never try too hard. Just act like you haven't put a lot of effort into it. Even though you have!"

Louis: "You can't go wrong with espadrilles and rolled up trousers."

Liam: "Actually I think you can never go wrong with a white T-shirt."

Harry: "Grow your hair and chuck stuff on and make it your own. As long as you feel good, you'll look good."

Any embarrassing fashion disasters you'd like to share?

Niall: "I used to wear tracksuits and had my ear pierced. I didn't have any fashion sense. I think I'm slightly better now. But I'm still a bit of a scruff."

Liam: "My hair straighteners are pink! I have to use them or my hair would be out of control. I also have highlights. I sit in the salon with my hair covered in foils in front of those massive granny heaters hoping no one recognizes me!"

Niall: "My hair was brown with stupid highlights before, but it got changed to bleached Eminem blond. I'm not going to lie, it hurt my scalp. I don't know how women do it."

Did you know: On *The X Factor* live tour, the playful bunch of scallywags decided to have some fun with their styling. Harry, Liam and Zayn donned some fake facial hair while Louis dressed as a giant carrot.

Liam says: "I'd love to shave my head one day. It's just so much work at the moment: washing it, drying it, straightening it and waxing it."

BABY PHOTOS!

Aren't they cute – can you guess who's who?

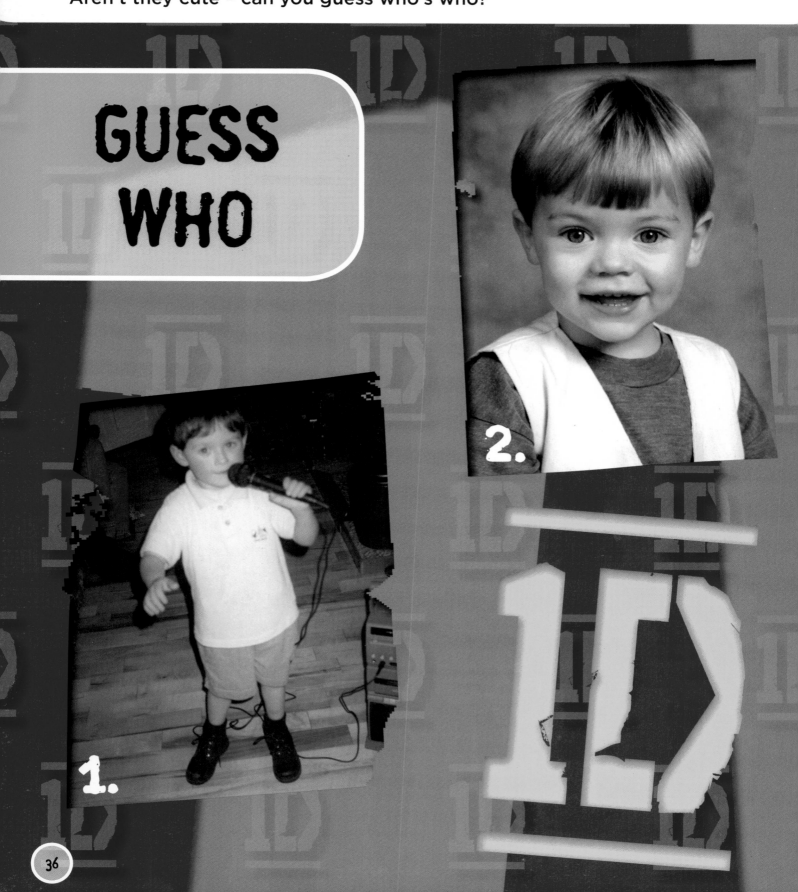

GUESS WHO

3.

4.

5.

WHO SAID WHAT?

Can you guess which of the 1D guys said the following?

1. "You can't turn up on stage with bruises."

2. "I'm the one who is 24/7 serious. Well, $23\frac{1}{2}/7$."

3. "Justin Bieber totally stole my hairstyle."

4. "Susan Boyle and Harry have exactly the same hair!"

5. "I thought we should all look like Louis because at the time I thought he looked really cool! How wrong I was!"

6. "I wasn't going to turn up for *The X Factor* audition but my mom basically grabbed me by the ear and told me I was doing it!"

7. "I can't dance to save my life."

8. "We're hoping to have a few parties."

9. "Emma Watson was my first-ever crush."

10. "I've been compared to Justin Bieber a few times and it's a comparison I like!"

Answers

1. Liam
2. Liam
3. Liam
4. Louis
5. Niall
6. Zayn
7. Zayn
8. Harry
9. Louis
10. Niall

HANGING WITH ONE DIRECTION

The guys chat to us about the *X Factor* tour, their new album and each other!

What were the best and worst bits of being on tour?

Zayn: "The best thing was performing. The worst things were the early mornings. We had to get up at about eight most mornings. I loved performing 'Grenade' every night. That was definitely my favorite track to perform."

Niall: "The best thing was playing to thousands of people every night and being part of such an amazing show. The worst thing was sitting around between shows. I get bored easily and get quite fidgety, so I always like having something to do."

Louis: "The good things were performing to so many people every night. Even if you woke up in a bad mood being on stage made you feel better. It was also great hanging out with everyone from *The X Factor*. We also gained a lot of confidence on the tour. The only bad thing was not being able to see my friends and family all the time and being away from home."

Harry: "The best bits were being on stage, and messing around while not on stage. The worst bits were being told where to go all the time because we were always busy."

Liam: "The best things were being on stage and all the performances, and the worst thing was that we didn't get many days off because we were working pretty much nonstop in between. It would have been nicer to get out and see the places we visited a bit more."

Do you have any funny stories to tell us about the tour?

Zayn: "We used to run through the crowd and Louis would give random things to the fans, like Nutri-Grain bars. One night he gave a fan 50 cents for no reason at all."

Niall: "We had a few fights in the dressing rooms. Also one time when Wagner from *The X-Factor* was asleep on the back of the tour bus Harry put loads of cuddly toys around him and took photos."

Louis: "I loved it when I went on stage in my carrot costume and we raised money for Help for Heroes. We also used to play this word game when we had to get some random words into the show – the best was 'winklepicker.'"

Liam: "I loved it when we kept shouting random words during the show. I shouted 'Del Boy' and 'Rodney' during 'Kids in America' one time."

"I'd love to work with Jessie J because I think she's incredible."

What was the best part about making the album?

Zayn: "I love being in the studio and hanging out with the other guys. I'm happiest when I'm in the studio."

Niall: "Getting to work in amazing studios and working with producers and songwriters that we could never have dreamed about working with before."

Louis: "It was great to go and record in different countries, and it was great fun filming our music video."

Harry: "Going to all of the different places to record and meeting all the people, and knowing that we were working on our first-ever album. It was amazing."

Liam: "Getting to see all the amazing things that go on behind the scenes. You also get to hear loads and loads of good music when you're in studios."

Any songs you'd particularly like to cover?

Zayn: "I've love to do a Bruno Mars track as I'm a big fan."

Niall: "I'd love to do a real cover of 'Grenade.' We've done an acoustic version on tour, but I'd love to do a proper one."

Louis: "I'd really love to do a Radio One *Live Lounge* doing something no one would ever expect us to do, like Dizzee Rascal's 'Bonkers.' I'd love to do something completely different to an original song."

Harry: "I'd like to do a version of 'Mr. Brightside' by The Killers because it can be done in so many different ways and I'd like to see how ours would turn out."

Liam: "'The 'Hokey Pokey' - it's always a group favorite."

Any artists you'd like to collaborate with in the near future?

Zayn: "Bruno Mars and Justin Timberlake, and I also really like Chris Brown. Any big names really."

Niall: "Bruno Mars would be a good one, and also Taio Cruz. Michael Bublé would be amazing even though he's swing and that's not our sound."

Louis: "My absolute idol is Robbie Williams, so we've already ticked that box by performing with him, but it would be great to actually record with him."

Harry: "I'd love to work with Jessie J because I think she's incredible."

Liam: "Taio Cruz. He makes great music one hundred percent of the time."

What advice would you give someone wanting to audition for *The X Factor*?

Zayn: "Think about what you're doing before you audition and think of every possible thing that can happen afterward. I didn't expect to get through and my life has been turned upside down. Make sure you consider actually getting through because your life changes. Take it all seriously."

Niall: "Keep your head down and be nice to everyone because the people that work there in the early stages will end up working with you later in the competition. Don't be overconfident going into your audition, choose your songs wisely and don't be generic."

Louis: "Be yourself and don't try and be someone you're not. Sell yourself, be confident and stand out from the crowd and choose your song well."

Harry: "Go for it. Be yourself and have fun with it because it's unbelievable."

Liam: "One hundred percent go for it and be ready for lots of hard work."

Do you still get nervous before a performance?

Zayn: "Yes, you can never escape your nerves. They're always there with you. Before *The X Factor* I used to get so nervous I'd feel sick and couldn't eat, but I'm not as bad now. Just before we go up on stage my stomach will start hurting, but once I'm up there I don't think about it as much. I enjoy it so much I just get on with it."

Niall: "Yes, all the time, especially on the *X Factor* tour. I always thought I'd fall over coming out of the elevator, but it was all good."

Louis: "Yes, definitely. I keep calm by standing on my own for a while and running through what we're doing in my head. Then just before we go on stage I get more excited than nervous."

Harry: "I do, but I take deep breaths, have a drink of water and chat to people around me to take my mind off of things."

Liam: "I do a little bit but not as much as I used to. Performing so often makes it much easier, and it's so much fun that I get more excited nervous than scary nervous."

You've met a lot of celebrities from the music and film industries — who was your favorite?

Zayn: "So many. Meeting Robbie Williams was amazing."

Niall: "Michael Bublé of course. We also met Alan Sugar, who was just like he was on the TV and said his family are fans of ours."

Louis: "Robbie Williams or Cheryl Cole. Robbie was so friendly, and Cheryl is an amazing girl and amazing to look at."

Harry: "Probably Simon Cowell. He's just a dude. He's a legend and he's so much funnier than people see on TV. We all got on really well with him."

Liam: "Michael McIntyre. He's such a nice guy and exactly like you see on TV. I thought he may put on a bit of a character but he doesn't at all. I did have his number but my phone managed to wipe everything and I'm gutted about it. We also met Russell Brand at *The X Factor* and he was hilarious. He's one of my favorite comedians."

Do you have any phobias?

Zayn: "I can't swim so I'm scared of water. I don't go near deep water because it makes me feel physically sick. Even if I look at the sea it makes me feel funny."

Niall: "I get a bit claustrophobic sometimes. When we came back from LA and there were all the girls at Heathrow airport that time, I didn't like it because I felt trapped."

Louis: "Yes. Ever since I was young I always had this paranoia about smelling of BO, so I smell myself all day. I never smell horrible, I always smell nice, but I worry about it."

Harry: "I used to be scared of roller coasters and big rides, then Louis took me on one on Brighton Pier so I think I've conquered my fear. That really helped me to get over it."

Liam: "Yes, spoons. I have to buy new ones or I can't use them. Even when I was little I didn't use spoons because I didn't like them."

Tell us about the rest of the band.

Zayn: "Louis is really funny, and Niall farts a lot, which can be really annoying when you're on a three-hour car journey. If I were to point out my own downsides I think I'm quite moody so you need to find the right time to crack a joke with me. Harry's just Harry, and Liam is just Liam. I don't get annoyed with any of them really."

Niall: "I like the way Louis is just out there, I like how Liam has turned into the funny one in the band, I love that Harry plays golf because we can go golfing together, and Zayn's a good laugh. The only thing we ever bicker about is where to eat. We genuinely get on really well. We're very tight."

Louis: "I like the way Niall is very laid-back and fun, Liam has become much more chilled out and he's a good laugh but he can also be serious, which is good. Zayn is quite similar to me. He's a risk taker so if I want to do something mischievous I'll ask him and he'll join me. Harry and I have loads in common. He's easygoing and easy to talk to and a good guy to be around. And he's got curly hair."

Harry: "I like the fact that we're all so different but we get on so well. I don't dislike anything specific, to be honest, or find anything annoying. I know that sounds a bit boring, but it's true. I love that we're all good at what we do individually and we've all got our roles."

Liam: "I like that Harry is cheeky all the time, Louis is always funny, I love that Niall's funny and I like trying to mimic his accent. Zayn is funny too, but he doesn't like losing so I don't like losing against him. I'm the most competitive out of all of us though. I think it's to do with my running when I was younger. I always like to win."

"I wouldn't want to be anyone else. I'm happy being me."

Which other member of the band would you like to be?

Zayn: "Liam, because he's the most similar to me and I'm pretty happy with who I am. Liam is pretty sensible and has a good outlook on life and always seems to see the rational side of things."

Niall: "I wouldn't want to be anyone else. I'm happy being me."

Louis: "I'd be a cross between Harry and Zayn. Zayn because he's perfect looking, and Harry because he's cheeky and he's a good guy."

Harry: "I guess Louis, because he has so much fun all the time and he's got a good outlook on life."

Liam: "I'd like to be Niall for the day because he's so carefree and fun. I'd also like to see what goes on inside his head, and I'd love to be able to do his accent really well."

Tell us one interesting thing we don't know about each of you.

Zayn: "Harry has got four nipples, Liam owns a pair of pink hair straighteners, Louis doesn't like anyone else wearing stripes, Niall's been teaching me guitar, and I can read Arabic."

Niall: "Zayn's got his ear pierced about seven times and he gets extra-hot sauce at Nando's. Sometimes Liam doesn't wear a T-shirt under his hoodie. Harry likes to get naked as everyone knows, and Louis only owns about two pairs of socks. As for me? I'm Irish! There's a good fact."

Louis: "Harry's got four nipples, Niall has a strange obsession with giraffes, Zayn is scared of shoelaces and can't have any shoes with laces in, and Liam enjoys flying kites in his spare time. The others will probably know some good ones about me."

Harry: "Liam straightens his hair every day, Niall once won supporter of the year at Derby County Football Club, Louis really likes his own bottom and Zayn really likes himself. And of course I've got four nipples, which is my classic chat-up line."

Liam: "I'm the tallest in the band at 5' 11", Harry has a big love for Abercrombie & Fitch, Louis owns the most clothes out of all of us, Zayn stays up the latest out of everyone and Niall's hair isn't naturally blond."

What are your New Year's resolutions for 2012?

Zayn: "I'm going to start going to the gym. I always say I'm going to do it and I never do. I say every year I'm going to put weight on and work out and I never do, so I'm determined!"

Niall: "To have a number one album and go on an arena tour."

Louis: "To keep making people laugh."

Harry: "I want to buy a classic car. I've always wanted one."

Liam: "To have a pet monkey like Ross from *Friends*. Everyone wants one, don't they? We all worked out who was who out of *Friends* the other day. I can't remember who all of us were, but I was Ross."

45

Quickfire Questions: Zayn

Instruments you play
I can play the guitar very roughly.

Favorite band or artist
I'd say Chris Brown.

Favorite TV show
When I was younger it was *Saved by the Bell*.

Favorite movie
Scarface

Favorite meal
Samosas or spaghetti Bolognese. It's the only thing I can cook.

Quickfire Questions: Liam

Instruments you play
A little bit of guitar and a little bit of piano, but I'm probably better at piano.

Favorite band or artist
*NSYNC, because they were pretty cool back in the day. And artists-wise, Taio Cruz.

Favorite TV show
Friends, still after all this time.

Favorite movie
The Toy Story films, and *Arthur*, the new one with Russell Brand. I thought it was hilarious.

Favorite meal
Mozzarella sticks are just the best. And I love cheeseburgers.

Quickfire Questions: Harry

Instruments you play
None. I once tried to learn the guitar but I gave up after a week.

Favorite band or artist
The Beatles and John Mayer

Favorite TV show
Family Guy

Favorite movie
I tell people it's *Fight Club*, but really it's *Titanic* and *Love Actually*.

Favorite meal
Tacos, and I love T.G.I. Friday's.

Quickfire Questions: Louis

Instruments you play
A little bit of piano. I taught myself about two years ago.

Favorite band or artist
The Fray and James Morrison

Favorite TV show
Skins, but the older series

Favorite movie
Grease. I've seen it a ridiculous amount of times.

Favorite meal
I love calzones, any pasta, and the cookie dough dessert from Pizza Hut.

Quickfire Questions: Niall

Instruments you play
I've played the guitar since I was about 12.

Favorite band or artist
Michael Bublé and The Script

Favorite TV show
Two and a Half Men

Favorite movie
Grease or *Big Daddy*

Favorite meal
Nando's

WHO'S YOUR FAVORITE?

Take our quiz and work out which 1D boy is for you...

1. ## What is your teacher most likely to say about you?

A. You're an incredibly hard worker
B. You need to speak up a bit more in class
C. There's more to school than organizing your social life
D. Less gossiping, more concentrating, please
E. You're always immaculately turned out

2. ## You arrive at your friend's house. What's the first thing you do?

A. Listen to her latest problem
B. Head to the kitchen for some snacks
C. Start discussing your crush
D. Reapply your lip gloss
E. Whatever your friend wants to do

3. ## What type of boy do you like?

A. Laid-back and easygoing
B. A serious softy
C. Cheeky with a side helping of charm
D. Good fun and good sense of humor
E. Someone who makes you LOL a lot

4. ## What would you wear on a first date?

A. A kitten-soft sweater
B. Your favorite jeans
C. Cute shorts
D. A stripy tee
E. A show-stoppin' outfit

5. ## If you were given $1,000, you'd:

A. Put it straight in the bank
B. Treat your family to something special
C. Buy your best friend a massive gift
D. Take your friends on a never-to-be-forgotten trip
E. Blow it all on a shopping trip

48

Mostly As? You could date...

Niall

Your dream date would be a laid-back perfect gent – just like Niall. You're super sweet and everyone knows they can rely on you. You always put other people's feelings first and are one of the nicest girls around!

Mostly Bs? You could date...

Liam

Secret softy Liam is the one for you. Like Liam you're a real romantic at heart and you have a wise head on your shoulders. You're also a bit of a shy girl and definitely like guys to make the first move.

Mostly Cs? You could date...

Harry

You're cheeky Harry's perfect match. You've got natural charm that attracts people to you. Girls want to be your friends and boys are dying to date you. With so much energy, you're bound to be a success.

Mostly Ds? You could date...

Louis

It looks like Louis may have met his match! You have a special talent of turning even the most boring day into a fun event. Everyone can't help but crack up at your silly pranks and the funny faces you make.

Mostly Es? You could date...

Zayn

A chic chick like you should be heading for a dream date with the sophisticated Zayn. Looking good on the outside makes you feel confident on the inside. You're a glam girl with your own hobbies and you're certainly no pushover.

A DATE WITH 1D

What would the One Direction guys be like as boyfriends?

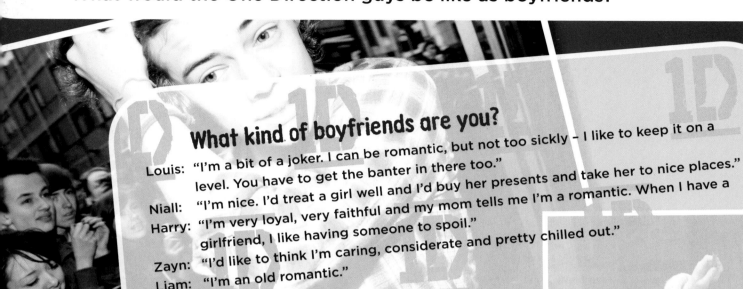

What kind of boyfriends are you?

Louis: "I'm a bit of a joker. I can be romantic, but not too sickly – I like to keep it on a level. You have to get the banter in there too."

Niall: "I'm nice. I'd treat a girl well and I'd buy her presents and take her to nice places."

Harry: "I'm very loyal, very faithful and my mom tells me I'm a romantic. When I have a girlfriend, I like having someone to spoil."

Zayn: "I'd like to think I'm caring, considerate and pretty chilled out."

Liam: "I'm an old romantic."

Where would you go on a date?

Louis: "I wouldn't try and be flashy, I'd just do something normal like go to the cinema and then to a nice Italian restaurant. I wouldn't want to go anywhere too posh, just somewhere where we can relax and eat nice food."

Niall: "I'd take her to Nando's because it's great. I'd want to do something quite fun. I don't think I'm super, super romantic, but I would make sure we had a good time."

Harry: "I'd take her to a restaurant where we can relax. We had dinner at The Ivy the other night and that was amazing, so I'd like to take someone there."

Zayn: "I'd probably take her out for a meal somewhere really nice and put a rose on the table. I'd do the whole wining and dining thing and make sure there's a lot of romance."

Liam: "I'd probably go to the cinema because I don't like small talk. I'm not Mr. Smooth. I'd probably just spot a girl with curly hair and ask her on a date to be honest!"

Would you pay for everything or share the bill?

Louis: "Oh no, I'd pay for everything."

Niall: "I'd definitely pay for everything."

Harry: "I would pay."

Zayn: "I'm a bit old-fashioned when it comes to things like that and I'd definitely pay for everything. I like to open doors for girls and that sort of thing, I like to feel as though I'm the protector."

Liam: "I would pay for everything."

What makes a good girlfriend?

Louis: "Someone who is loyal and has a sense of humor, and is kindhearted too. Oh, and if they were tidy, that would be good, because I'm not."

Niall: "I like someone who can take a bit of banter."

Harry: "A good sense of humor and someone who is loyal and cute. I like cute girls."

Zayn: "I find a girl acting cool attractive. I like a girl who knows what she wants and makes me work for her."

Liam: "Someone who's cheeky but quiet too. A bit shy as well. I don't really like loud girls. I like happy, smiley girls."

Is there a certain type of girl that you go for?

Louis: "I don't think so, no, but I like someone who likes a laugh."

Niall: "I don't mind – they can be blonde, as long as they're not blonde, if you get me!"

Harry: "I don't have a hair color type, but I do love cute girls."

Zayn: "I go for brunettes with olive skin and brightly colored eyes. Eyes play a big part in my decision."

Liam: "I like mousy brown-haired girls."

Finally, who's your celebrity crush?

Louis: "I would like to go on a date with someone like Diana Vickers. I've met her a few times and she seems quite cool and fun."

Niall: "Cheryl Cole. She's very nice and she's a great laugh, she's just like your average girl."

Harry: "Frankie Sandford. I've met her and she's a lovely girl."

Zayn: "I haven't met them yet, so who knows? I'm sure I'll find out one day."

Liam: "Leona Lewis or the curly haired girl who used to be on the Marks & Spencer ads (model Noémie Lenoir). I definitely have a type."

LIVE YOUR LIFE THE 1D WAY!

Can't get enough of the guys? Well, spend a day living like them!

1. Listen to The Beatles – Harry's favorite band.
   Put them on your MP3 player so you can have a bit of Harry wherever you go.

2. Organize your room – Zayn style. Make sure you hide any Birkenstock sandals or granny cardigans – Niall can't stand them.

3. Make some One Direction masks to show your 1D love.

4. Watch the Toy Story movies back-to-back. They're Liam's fave films!

5. Sing "She's the One" by Robbie Williams on karaoke and reminisce about that fateful *X Factor* final.

6. Head out to Nando's – it's where Zayn celebrated his 18th birthday party with the boys!

7. Spend an hour signing autographs for your friends and family.

8. Curl your hair à la Harry.

9. Eat a bowl of sweet corn. If Harry could survive on only one vegetable, that's the one he'd choose!

10. Learn some jokes and make people laugh like Louis.

11. Play on Pokémon – the boys are all big fans.

12. Make yourself a T-shirt that says: I STOLE LIAM'S HAIR.

13. Shape One Direction out of a box of carrots. Liam says, "We got sent a box of carrots the other day with all our faces drawn on. As I'm the tallest, I was the biggest and Niall was the tiny one – they had cut his carrot in half!"

14. Take your brother to the hairdresser and ask for a Zayn.

15. Dab some Hollister under your nose and smell like Louis all day.

16. Stick on a fake tattoo. Liam loves 'em.

ONE DIRECTION AND YOU

If there's one thing the boys are grateful for, it's their fans.

You have such amazing fans – what's the nicest thing a fan has ever done for you?

Zayn: "A fan painted a really good picture of me recently. One fan also found out what my favorite aftershave was and gave me some. It was really expensive and it was very cool. Harry always tweets that he likes Haribo and I put that I like Skittles, so we get given loads of those."

Niall: "They stay out really late just to catch a glimpse of us, and they give you great presents. They always give me socks and boxers so I don't have to go shopping for them."

Louis: "I can't put my finger on one thing. I just think it's amazing when people travel from all over the country to come and see us. The commitment they have is amazing."

Harry: "A fan lent me her student card so I could get money off a laptop. She saved me a lot of money, so I gave her my iPod. I think she was quite happy with it."

Liam: "I saw a picture someone drew of me in a Buzz Lightyear costume which was really cool."

Who gets the most female attention?

Zayn: "I'd say it was Harry from the younger audience, but when it comes to the older audience we all have our own fans I think. Harry's got the cheeky appeal for the younger fans."

Niall: "We all know the answer to this! Harry. It's not something we ever argue over or anything though!"

Louis: "Harry Styles. If I was a One Direction fan I would definitely fancy Harry. He's got that cheeky personality and that curly hair and he's a good-looking guy."

Harry: "I don't know. I think we all get our fair share and all the fans are brilliant."

Liam: "I would say Harry, but I think if you like one person in the band, you'll like another one too. There's a good mix in the group."

What's the best or strangest thing you've ever been given by a fan?

Zayn: "We get some strange things like knickers from some fans and some carrots with our faces on."

Niall: "The weirdest thing we were given was a box full of mushrooms that had beady eyes on them and hair to make them look like us."

Louis: "I was given carrots everywhere I go because I said in a video I like girls who eat carrots."

Harry: "Someone recently painted us a massive canvas of the five of us and that was very cool."

Liam: "The weirdest things have to be the boxes of vegetables we get. It's Louis's fault because he said he liked carrots."

What do you think of your fans?

Louis: "We wouldn't be here now if it wasn't for the fans who voted for us. We've received letters and amazing pictures that people have drawn. They've made such an effort. When you arrive somewhere and people are cheering and shouting your name, anyone would love it."

Harry: "We feel like we're five of the luckiest boys in the world and we just want to say a huge thank-you to all the fans."

Niall: "It was you who got us here, and we won't ever forget it."

ONE DIRECTION

THE FUTURE

Right now, the future's so bright the boys must be pinching themselves on a regular basis to make sure they're not dreaming!

None of them could have imagined how much their lives would change in such a short time. With their first album, Harry, Louis, Liam, Niall and Zayn are ready to take things to another level. It's destined to be one of the albums of the year and shows how much the boys have grown as artists since we first saw them on our screens.

One Direction have an incredibly healthy attitude to pop stardom. Despite their whirlwind success, the boys have managed to keep their egos and their sense of humor in check.

"There's far too much banter in this group for it ever to go to our heads," laughs Louis.

Harry agrees, "As soon as someone gets a bit diva, the rest of the band are on them."

It's no longer possible for the five guys to live a "real" life, what with the demands on their waking hours, plane trips across continents and round after round of interviews. But they've managed to embrace all the hard work with good grace and hang on to a sense of fun.

Knowing the boys, they are going to be here for a long time to come. They know the music business is risky, but they have more than enough talent and the right work ethic to see them through.

As Liam says, "We look at other bands and see how successful they've been. We want some of that for ourselves and we're willing to work as hard as we need to in order to achieve it. Bring it on!"

The ball is certainly rolling and there's no way to stop it now. One Direction's schedule has been mapped out in detail for the next year. But the boys wouldn't change a single thing. They're determined to make their mark and along the way influence a whole new generation of bands. They're blazing a trail, not only for themselves but for all the bands that will undoubtedly follow them.

They've made the kind of start that's labeled them as *X Factor* legends. Their ambition and determination will carry them wherever they choose to go. Above all else they've shown it's possible to make dreams come true and achieve your heart's desire. They've given us everything and they won't stop for a long, long time to come!

"We look at other bands and see how successful they've been. We want some of that for ourselves and we're willing to work as hard as we need to in order to achieve it. Bring it on!"

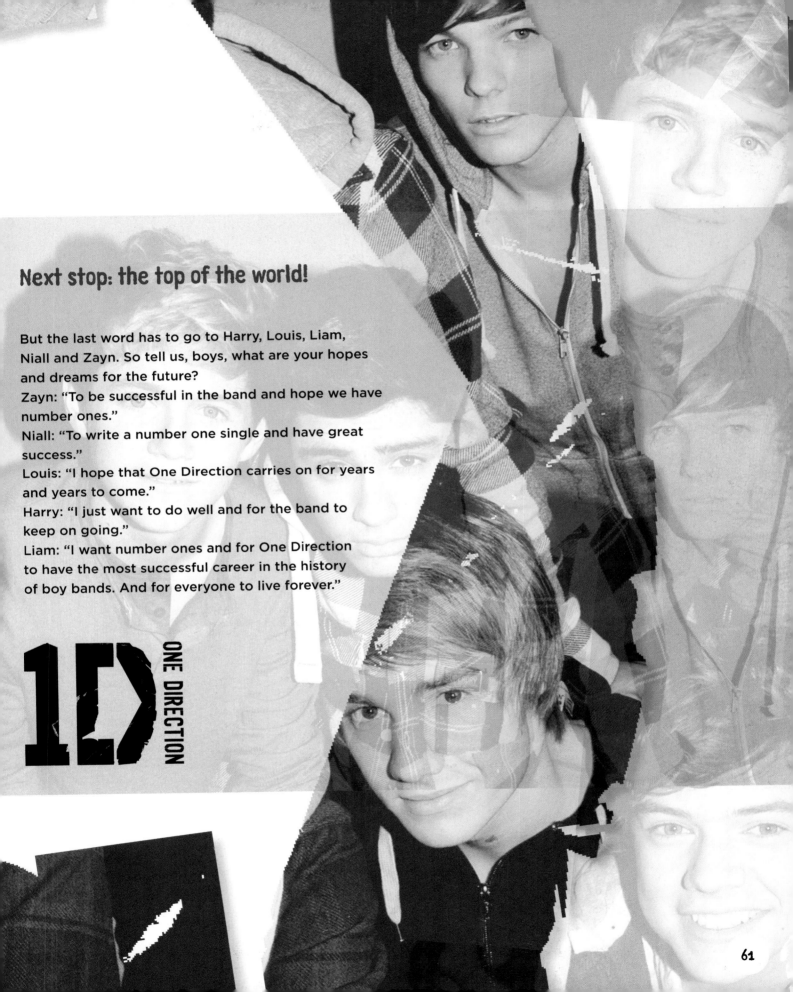

Next stop: the top of the world!

But the last word has to go to Harry, Louis, Liam, Niall and Zayn. So tell us, boys, what are your hopes and dreams for the future?

Zayn: "To be successful in the band and hope we have number ones."

Niall: "To write a number one single and have great success."

Louis: "I hope that One Direction carries on for years and years to come."

Harry: "I just want to do well and for the band to keep on going."

Liam: "I want number ones and for One Direction to have the most successful career in the history of boy bands. And for everyone to live forever."

1D ONE DIRECTION

Liam x

Louis !!
x

Harry

Zayn x

Niall